The Ultimate HOW-TO-DRAW REAL STUFF Book

Illustrated by Kelley Cunningham

SCHOLASTIC INC.

NEW YORK   TORONTO   LONDON   AUCKLAND   SYDNEY
MEXICO CITY   NEW DELHI   HONG KONG   BUENOS AIRES

ISBN 0-439-81336-0

Published by Scholastic Inc.

SCHOLASTIC and associated logos are trademarks
and/or registered trademarks of Scholastic Inc.

12 11 10 9 8 7 6 5 4 3 2 1   5 6 7 8 9 10/0

Printed in the U.S.A.
First Scholastic printing, February 2006

Table of
Contents

Welcome to Realistic Drawing 4

SEEING With Your Eyes Closed 8

Hands + Eyes + the Right Side of Your Brain 12

The Shape of Things 14

Look Carefully! 18

When the Negative Is Good 19

Making New Friends: Drawing People 20

Drawing Boys 29

Working with Ink and Brush 37

Drawing the Great Outdoors 38

Drawing from Your Imagination 46

WELCOME TO REALISTIC DRAWING

When your drawing looks like the real thing—that's realistic drawing. Some artists draw so realistically that what they draw looks like a photo. In this book we'll explore the methods that will help you draw objects, living things, and landscapes so they appear real.

You'll learn how to break things into shapes for easier, more accurate drawing. You will discover ways of "seeing" the outline of something. You'll find step-by-step instructions for drawing people and landscapes. And you'll learn helpful hints to make your drawings look even more real.

To become a good "realistic" artist you're going to need artists' skills, and that doesn't mean just the tricks for how to make things look real. You'll need eyes that see, and hands that draw, and a lively imagination. Think of this book as a friend. Inside it you'll find a special (and magical) guide to help you become a better artist. With patience and practice, you'll be on your way to becoming an artist who knows how to draw realistically! Ready to get started? Let's go!

Your Amazing New Supplies

Here is your art supply kit. With your kit you will be able to draw anything you can think of. You shall draw new friends, create fantastic places to go, things to do and see. An amazing world in art awaits you.

THREE CHARCOALS
(one light, one medium, one dark)

BLACK INK

TWO BRUSHES

KNEADED ERASER

SKETCHPAD

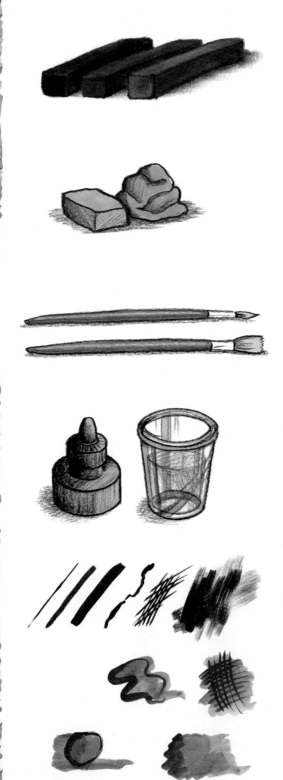

CHARCOAL: Charcoal is really messy and really smudgy, so if you're right-handed try to draw from left to right and if you're left-handed from right to left. That way you won't keep rubbing your hand over what you've drawn already.

KNEADED ERASER: You can play with it like putty—pull it apart, squeeze it in your hands, rip it into little pieces, and put it back together again! Use it to erase all the stuff you don't like. It can create light areas in your drawings, too. This is great for making things look realistic!

INK BRUSHES: Use them with the black ink. Always wash them gently with soap and water when you're done working with the ink, and use your fingers to bring the bristles to a point. Make sure to let them dry either lying flat or bristles up in the air. NEVER close them in a box when they're damp.

BLACK INK: You really need to make sure you've covered your work area when you use ink because it STAINS. Ink is cool because it can be used like a paint—and it will be very dark—or you can dilute it with water.

Here's how: take a little plastic cup, put a teeny bit of ink in it and then—slowly—add drops of water until it's a darkness that you like. Experiment! You can make lines or whole areas of dark or light color. Look below for examples of ways you can use ink.

USES FOR INK: With ink you can make lines of different widths, shapes, and textures. Ink washes can be light or dark. They can help you shade and add depth.

SKETCHPAD: Don't forget that you have a great, new, green sketchpad in your kit. A sketchpad is someplace to save your ideas and watch how much you've grown as an artist. May you have many, many more!

SEEING WITH YOUR EYES CLOSED

Walk into your bedroom, stop for one second, close your eyes really tightly. Can you picture your room? How many drawers are in your dresser? What's on top of the dresser? What's on the floor? Is it messy or neat? And if you opened your eyes this very minute, could you draw it—the whole room—just the way it is? Would it look exactly like your room? Or would it be slightly changed?

When you pictured your room, you probably left out some things. Did you include every wall outlet? Each book and poster? The things you didn't remember when you closed your eyes are, most likely, not as important to you as the things you did remember.

Any time you look at a picture, like a room or an outdoor scene, notice what you find interesting. Include those things in your artwork. Leave out what doesn't interest you. In this way—even though your art will be realistic—it will also reflect something about you, the artist.

Same Subject, Three Approaches

As we talked about on the last page, three artists will draw the same thing three different ways. Take this still-life, for instance. (A picture of things—not people—is called a still life.) Notice how each artist does something different with it!

This is the photo that the three artists used to make their artwork.

Christine Frerichs used detailed line work to make her art look real. Notice how she used lines to shade the potatoes and make them seem rounded.

Kelley Cunningham's drawing is very realistic. She made the surface of the book even darker than in the photo. Notice how real the cauliflower in the back is.

Joanne Penna made her painting lighter than the photo. She showed many details of the pattern on the ceramic cat and highlighted the worn spots on the book.

No two artists will ever draw this cat the same exact way. Drawing is just a bunch of lines on a flat surface. Look at this simple line drawing of the photo on page 6—just lines on a page, right? But our artists used color, dimension, shading, and detail to make it interesting. In short, they each added DRAMA to the subject in their own way! It's that certain *something* in you that makes you unique that will also make your realistic drawings unique!

Set Up Your Own Still Life

A great way to learn is to take a look at what's been done before. The artists Caravaggio, Vermeer, and Cezanne all made a painting of fruit on a table. You can find their paintings in an encyclopedia, in your library, or online. Do they look alike? Each one is realistic, but did you ever think pictures of fruit on a table could be *so* different from one another?

Start thinking about still lives that you might like to draw or paint one day. You can group together objects of any kind—your favorite stuffed animals, candies, your robot collection. Just have a blast placing your stuff in different ways. You can even snap photos of your set-ups so that you can remember them later on!

HANDS + EYES + THE RIGHT SIDE OF YOUR BRAIN

Scientists have a theory that people learn things differently from one another. People use both sides of their brain, but some people favor the left side of the brain and other people favor the right side of the brain. The left side is the part that figures out math problems and science experiments. It's logical. Orderly. The right side is the creative half.

For drawing, even realistic drawing, we need to tap into the right side of the brain. Your hands, your eyes, and your brain all work together to make your art happen.

The very best way to get your hands thinking for themselves is through a totally fun art exercise called blind drawing. It's a game that you can do on your own or, for extra fun, with a friend or family member. Grab whoever's nearest and give this a try.

Here's what you'll need: lots of paper, a pencil, pen or fine-tipped marker, and a kitchen timer.

Sit down with your partner, either on the floor or at a table. Set your timer for 3 minutes. Now, without looking down at your paper—EVER—you and your partner are going to draw each other—at exactly the same time. DO NOT CHEAT, DO NOT LOOK DOWN! Until the bell rings, of course. Then you can look down and laugh yourselves silly!

Once you understand how blind drawing works, you can try taking turns. Or you can do blind drawings of anything, anywhere, whenever you want. Not just people. You can do it with a timer or without a timer. You can change the number of minutes to make it faster or slower. Have fun doing your blind drawings and before you know it, your drawings will be a million times better!

THE SHAPE OF THINGS

Now let's put that logical left brain to work. To draw well you'll need to be able to quickly identify the shapes that things are made of. Try this experiment: hold your hand out in front of you with the palm away from your face. What shape do you see? How about a diamond? See? Your hand is narrow at the wrist, wide across the knuckles and then narrow again on top. It's a diamond shape! Take a look at the picture on the next page and see if you can find the big shapes on your own. Then turn the page to see the answers.

How many shapes did you get? All of them?

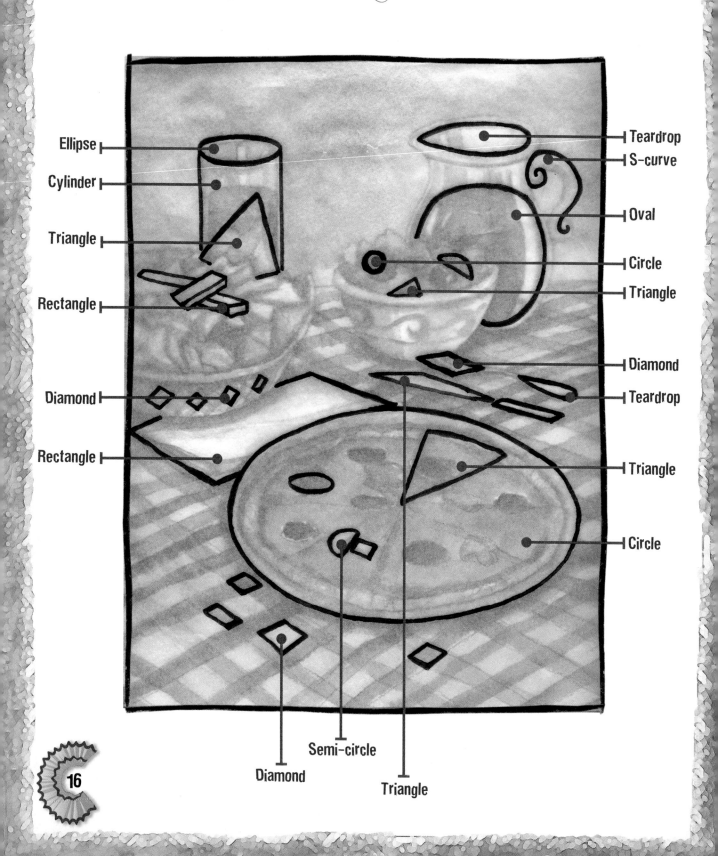

Ellipse

Cylinder

Triangle

Rectangle

Diamond

Rectangle

Teardrop

S-curve

Oval

Circle

Triangle

Diamond

Teardrop

Triangle

Circle

Semi-circle

Diamond

Triangle

Seeing Shapes Everywhere

How do artists draw what appear to be 3-dimensional shapes (often called 3-D)—shapes with thickness and roundness—on a 2-dimensional (meaning flat, often called 2-D) surface? They do it by knowing what flat shapes to use to make something look like it's 3-D. Some 2-D shapes are: circle, triangle, rectangle, square, and diamond. Some 3-D shapes are: cylinder, sphere, cube, and cone.

For some examples of how this works, take a look below.

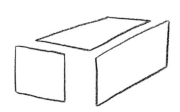 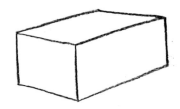 

Take a look at the tissue box shapes: 1 diamond and 2 slanted rectangles joined together in a very wide V shape. That's because we're looking at the edge of the box.

Take a careful look at where the lines around the box are thicker and thinner. They get really dark to show where the box is touching the table.

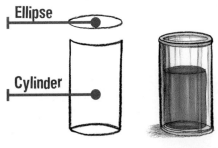

This glass is a cylinder. The flattened out circle at the top of the glass is called an ellipse. Check out the top of the glass—when the ellipse is above your eye-level it curves upwards in an arc. And at the bottom of the glass—which is below your eye level—it curves down!

Even a dog can be broken down into its shapes. How many triangles can you find in the dog's head?

LOOK CAREFULLY!

We often draw what we think we see instead of what's really there. If someone asked you to draw a cat, you might draw a picture that looks something like this:

Is this what a cat really looks like? Not really. When you draw a cat without looking at the real animal it can come out having a cartoonish quality to it.

Many times our idea of what something looks like changes once we really look at it carefully. One way to start seeing a thing more accurately is to study its outline. Contour drawing to the rescue. Draw the cat's outline without picking up your pencil. The next time you want to draw something, take a moment to study its outline. Most likely you'll discover a new way of seeing that thing.

This sleeping cat forms a sort of oval and its legs flop lazily. Try drawing a sleeping animal yourself. (Most pets won't stay still if they're awake.)

HERE ARE SOME MORE REALLY HELPFUL TIPS!

Let's say you decide to draw a box. You draw, draw, draw and...Ta Da! A box! Everything around and outside of the box—all that white "empty" paper—is called the negative space. A real artist needs to think very carefully about what goes on in the negative space because it affects the way we see the object. If the negative space is black, the box looks one way; if the negative space is pink, the box looks completely different. Imagine if the negative space were filled with polka dots . . . .

You might think there is nothing around this box, but look at it another way. It really has writing and other artwork around it. What's OUTSIDE THE BOX is as important as the box itself.

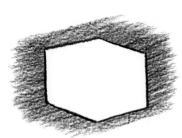

Here's the black background with the box taken out. Imagine the box back inside. Would the red stand out more? Does the darkness make you think it's in a room or outside? Does it make you think of day or night?

What if we put our box in this background? Does it seem to be floating in some fantasy land? Does it affect what you think about the box and what might be in it?

MAKING NEW FRIENDS
DRAWING PEOPLE

THESE ARE CRAZY COOL BOX SEATS. BUT WHAT ARE WE GOING TO SEE?

AN EXCITING NEW STAR IS ABOUT TO BE BORN OR MAYBE I SHOULD SAY, ABOUT TO BE DRAWN.

Do you want to draw a rock star? Or a new friend? Maybe you just want to draw a picture of your little sister. But first you have to know a little something about drawing real people. Let's start learning how to draw one fun-loving and friendly girl. She's sure to be the star of the show.

DRAWING a HEAD

Let's start from the top. The first thing you'll need is a nice egg-shaped oval: bigger on top for the brain and smaller on the bottom for the chin. Next come the guidelines. Guidelines are what artists use to make sure that all the parts of the face are where they should be. Guidelines should be drawn very lightly. Once you've got the parts of the face drawn in you will be erasing all your guidelines.

The Guidelines

STEP 1: Divide the whole face in half. The eyes are on that line.

STEP 2: Then divide the bottom half of the face in half again. That's your nose line.

STEP 3: Divide the bottom space in half and you have the mouth line!

The Vertical Line (Up-and-Down)

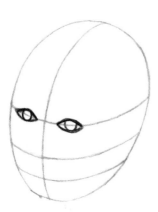

You'll also need an up and down guideline since faces are the same on both sides. Notice that line in this picture isn't in the center because this face is turned $3/4$ to the left. It's called a $3/4$ profile, so vertical guideline is $3/4$ to the left.

DRAWING an EYE

STEP 1: Draw an almond shape. (Outside)

STEP 2: Draw two curved lines inside. (Pupil)

STEP 3: Add a smaller circle in the center and line above. (Iris) Put a line above for an eyelid.

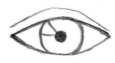

STEP 4: Add a little white triangle for shine. (Light)

STEP 5: Fill in the iris with soft lines.

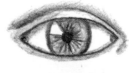

STEP 6: Add shading.

STEP 7: The eyelashes follow the curve of the eye.

Remember, when you're drawing a $3/4$ profile, the eyes will be at a $3/4$ angle, too.

DRAWING the EAR

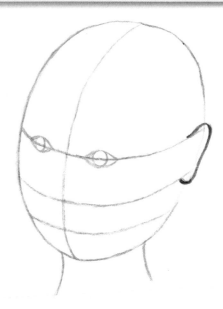

 STEP 1: The ear is a bit like a backwards C. Everyone's ears are a bit different.

 STEP 2: Another C shape inside.

 STEP 3: Hook that shape to a squiggle backwards C.

 STEP 4: Add a little bump and you've got your basic structure.

 STEP 5: Now it's time for shading. Wherever you have a deep hole or crease, the shading is going to be darkest. Where it sticks out, it's lightest.

The top of the ear goes just a smidgen above the eye line. Most of it is between your mouth and your nose.

DRAWING the NOSE

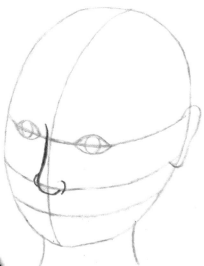

 STEP 1: Draw a circle for the bulb of the nose. And then add a half circle for the nostril on the far side.

 STEP 2: Add a backward C with a looped bottom on the nearest side.

STEP 3: Add a curved line for the nose bone.

 STEP 4: Start shading the bulb of the nose, the nostrils, and the nose bone.

 STEP 5: Erase the top line of the bulb. Darken the inner nostril.

The nose is tricky because it doesn't have the same kind of hard edges that the ear or eyes have.

DRAWING the MOUTH

Remember, when you're drawing a $^3/_4$ profile, the mouth will be at a $^3/_4$ angle, too.

STEP 1: Start from the midline and lightly draw the shape between the two lips.

STEP 2: Add a lima bean shape right from the middle of that line before it begins to slope down.

STEP 3: Three little circles will mark the plumper areas of the top lip. Largest in the center and two smaller ones that sit on the points.

STEP 4: Now draw the top of mouth. You'll get a great, natural shape as you trace around your little circles.

STEP 5: Draw the outline of the bottom lip.

STEP 6: Now shade in the top lip. Shade the bottom of the middle circle just the way you did the bulb of the nose.

STEP 7: There are little vertical lines on the surface of your lips? Draw them in.

STEP 8: Finish your shading.

DRAWING the HAIR

Start at the scalp and shoot those hairs downward in a nice stroke. Since the hair gets softer and more pointy as it gets to the ends, start with more pressure at the scalp and then take the pressure off as you get to the end of each hair. To make hair shiny use an eraser, right where the head starts to curve downwards.

SHADOWS and HIGHLIGHTS

STEP 1: To make the egg look more like a head and less like an egg, make sure to indent under the brow bone, and give a more human shape to the chin.

Every face grows out of an egg shape. Of course each egg shape is different, just like each of us is different. And there is no perfect oval head. Take a look around you if you're not sure.

STEP 2: Dimensionality—making things look as if they're not flat—comes from shading. Work gently with your pencil to build up layers of shadow. See how the face is darkest around the edges, lighter as you come toward the middle and then light in the center.

YOU DEFINITELY NEED A BODY!

Hmm, there's definitely a good part of this young lady missing! We need to draw a body for her. But how?

To make a great, realistic-looking body, you've got to have an idea about the way all the body parts fit together. Stick figures, the very kind you used to draw in kindergarten, are a great tool. You use sticks for the bones and circles for the joints. That way you can tell which parts of the body bend and which parts don't. If that sounds strange, you'll get a better idea of how this works in the coming pages. So turn the page.

STICK FIGURES AND INSTRUCTIONS COMING UP!

Start with STICKS and SHAPES

STEP 1: To begin the body, you need the head! Add the spine starting right from the base of the skull. Your spine goes from your skull to your hips! Make big circles for the hips and little ones for the knees. Make triangles for the feet.

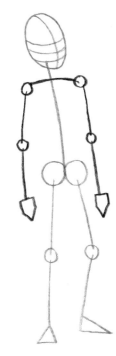

STEP 2: The shoulders are slightly wider than the head and the hands —shaped like little upside down houses. They hang down to the middle of the thigh bone. Look carefully: you can see that one arm is straighter than the other.

A BIG TIP

The head is important since the size of the entire body depends upon the size of the head. Grown-ups are usually 7 heads tall. Kids are only 6 heads.

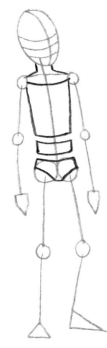

STEP 3: Now add the big, basic body shapes. A nice slope from the skull to the shoulders. Notice how the body is wider on the top and narrower at the bottom, and curved at both ends like a cylinder. The mid-section is rectangular, but also curved, and the bottom part is somewhat like a triangle with the hip balls sticking out of the bottom.

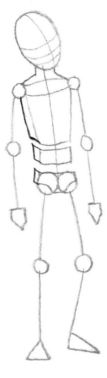

STEP 4: To the left of each of the big body shapes add a parallel line; then connect those to the body using two slightly diagonal lines. Here's a tip: if you can't figure out how to make the lines on your page look like the ones here, use a fingertip or your pencil to lightly trace over the drawing in this book. Do it a few times and you'll quickly get the hang of it!

STEP 5: Flesh out the arms and legs with basic rectangles. See how the rectangles are joined to the stick figure with a diagonal line? Take your pencil again and lightly trace over each of the figures until your hand knows just what to do.

STEP 6: Add a matching set of lines on the opposite side of each body part. See how the tops of the arms and legs join the bond with a pointy shape?

STEP 7: Carefully trace around everything you've drawn. Let the line indent a bit where you've got your circles and at other joining spots and lo and behold, you've got a flesh and blood body! (Or at least a drawing that looks like one!)

STEP 8: Erase all the lines inside the body. Now that you have the body weight and the way she's standing worked out, you can give her some clothes.

STEP 9: A couple of simple details—a necklace, a belt, pockets and shoes give her that "realistic" look. Notice again how everything on the page is related to a very basic shape— oval for the necklace, triangles and rectangle for the belt, blunt triangles for the shoes.

A BIG TIP   The body is like a **cylinder.**

STEP 10: Erase all the inside lines again and now shade in the body. Make it darkest near the sides, medium dark as you move towards the middle, and gradually lighter and lighter until you get to the center, which is white. Look at how the white highlight follows the shape of the thing it's part of. One pant leg is triangular and so is its highlight. The other leg is more rectangular and so is its highlight.

DRAWING BOYS

There are some differences when drawing a boy and drawing a girl. A boy's ears are usually bigger. Often his shoulders are wider and his hips are narrower. Follow the step-by-steps on the next pages and let's put a boy in the picture.

The Boy's HEAD

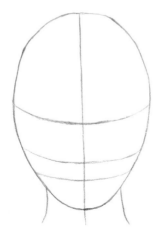

STEP 1: Drawing the boy's head is the same as drawing the girl's head. Notice, though, that unlike the girl, this time our boy is facing straight forward. Begin with your light guidelines: vertically divide the face in half, then horizontally in half (that's the eyeline), then the bottom in half (the nose line).

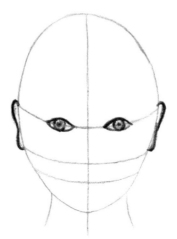

STEP 2: Add the eyes and ears. The boy's ears are a bit bigger than the girl's. Bet you can't see the inside of his ears the way we could the girl's! That's because he's facing us. That's just one of the differences between drawing someone head on, or drawing them in $3/4$ view.

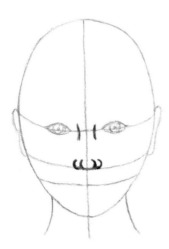

STEP 3: Draw 2 lines between the eyes. Then add a shallow U on the nose line surrounded by friendly half curves that extend just a bit down from the U.

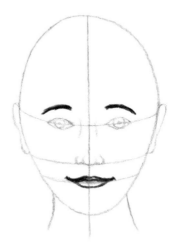

STEP 4: Boys have thicker, straighter brows than most girls. Lips are simple: draw the top lip right on the line. Leave a little space, and then add a shallow curve that doesn't touch the corners.

TIPS FOR USING YOUR CHARCOAL

By pressing harder or softer with your charcoal, you can get a big variety in the kinds of line and color in your drawing. Charcoal is great for shading. Try smudging your lines with a Q-tip or your fingers. Then take your kneaded eraser to create really white spots where you want highlights.

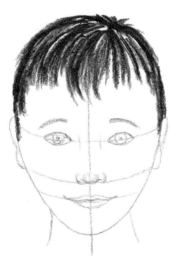

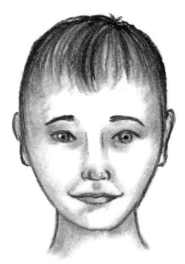

STEP 5: This guy's too young to be bald, so give him some hair. Start from a point on the right side of his scalp and move those lines down his head. Leave a few short hairs sticking up in a cowlick. Everyone's got them. Even girls! It's very natural looking.

STEP 6: Here's where you can adjust the chin: square it off a bit to give him character. And now for some finger fun: shade away! (Or use a Q-tip.) Look back at the drawing of the shaded egg on page 24 to remember what shading looks like when there's no face there.

DRAWING the Boy's BODY

STEP 1: Circles for the hips and the knees, triangles for the feet.

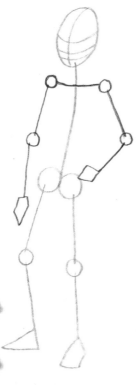

STEP 2: Shoulders slope down in the middle and are a little wider than his head. Every joint gets a bendy ball. And the hands are like little diamonds or upside down houses.

STEP 3: Let's fill this dude out. A pair of parallel lines for the neck goes half-way to the shoulder dip. Finish the neck with a rounded bottom (It's that old cylinder again!) From there two lines down to the shoulders form a triangle. Now add the body: torso, waist, and pelvis.

STEP 4: Time to build the body box. Add a parallel line in each of the areas shown and join to the body on a slight diagonal. That makes him begin to be dimensional.

STEP 5: Now let's be even more 3-D-ish. Each body part needs to be fleshed out. Notice how the parallel lines join to the stick figure on an angle.

STEP 6: We can't have him be lopsided, so do the other side too. He looks pretty 3-D now, wouldn't you say? See how we've left space around his joint circles. They look like spheres now that they're surrounded by the 3-D body boxes!

STEP 7: And now, once again, THE EASY PART! Go ahead and connect the parts. Notice how the hands become kind of mitteny.

STEP 8: And now, erase all that stuff and give him some clothes.

STEP 9: Erase the leg lines from inside the shorts and start filling in the clothing. This is a great time to add his face. Use what you've learned from drawing the girl to help you give him a $3/4$ profile. Remember the cylinder as you're coloring in his shorts.

STEP 10: And now shade and shadow. If you're using fingers, just remember you've got 10 of them. Pinkies can be very useful too. And so are Q-tips and your kneaded eraser.

DRAWING the HANDS

Let's take a closer look at this boy's hands. How many great pictures have you drawn where the hands just looked like weird bricks? Follow this simple diagram to get a handle on the hand!

STEP 1: Draw a small square, then add a parallel line and connect with diagonals, just like you did in the body boxes. This is the wrist.

STEP 2: Now you're going to need an extension for the back of the hand. Narrow at the bottom, broad at the top.

STEP 3: And just the opposite for the fingers. An extension that's broad at the base and narrow at the top.

STEP 4: Off to the left add a thumb joint. It's just a narrow rectangle. Then another rectangle with a slightly rounded top aims a bit back toward the hand for the top of the thumb. Extend a small line down from that rectangle to creates some space between the thumb and fingers.

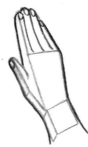

STEP 5: Divide the hand into 4 fingers. Remember that the middle finger is longest. Add some nails.

STEP 6: Erase all your internal lines and begin shading and shaping the fingers.

STEP 7: Look at your own fingernails. See how the "moon" at the base is lighter than the rest of the nail? How it's kind of streaky and darker around the cuticle? Use your kneaded eraser for highlights.

STEP 8: You can think of the fingers like sausages. Use shading to make the creases in the skin over the knuckles. Look at your own hands. Do the knuckle creases line up in one straight line? No they don't ! Always check things out for yourself.

DRAWING the FEET

STEP 1: Build your box.

STEP 2: Add a small circle on the left hand side of the box.

STEP 3: Add a bigger circle right underneath that one.

STEP 4: Now another almost box: a triangle with no point and a rectangle with no 4th side.

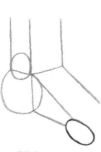

STEP 5: Close the triangle off with an oval.

STEP 6: And close the long rectangle off with another rectangle.

STEP 7: Add the big toe box. It's like an L. Take the time trace this shape with your fingers and your pencil so that your hands memorize it.

STEP 8: Close off the end of the foot. It will look almost like a little house that's listing to one side. Why? Because the toes get shorter as they get smaller!

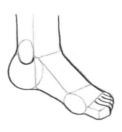

STEP 9: You're almost there . . . trace around the entire shape. Be sure to underscore the bottom of the first little circle you drew. That will be the ankle. Separate the house into toes.

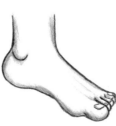

STEP 10: Erase your guidelines. And shade away. Don't forget the toenails!

WORKING WITH INK AND BRUSH

WHAT'S THIS? INK AND A BRUSH?

Now that you've learned to see shapes and draw people, let's take things outdoors and see what we can do. Only, for this section, let's try working with pen and ink. A brush and ink may seem a bit unusual to us now, but check out art from the old days when tons of stuff was done with ink and a brush. It's very cool stuff and you can add all kinds of great effects to your artwork.

Dip a dry brush in ink and you get a nice thick, black line. If you use a wet brush, or put a little water in your ink, you'll get a softer kind of line or a paler, see-through area of color. That's called a wash.

If you twist the brush while you're using it and change the pressure on it you'll get this cool, swirly kind of line.

You can create a great effect when you outline in pencil and then put an ink wash over it. That's what we did in this drawing of a box.

37

DRAWING THE GREAT OUTDOORS

Putting Things in Perspective

Artists use a trick called perspective—which means seeing through—to make the things they draw look like things, not just flat blobs.

Take these balls for instance. When they're lined up in a row they all seem the same size. But when we line them up one behind the other the front one looks the biggest, the one behind it smaller and the one behind it even smaller. Try it out with real balls on a flat surface and you'll see what we mean.

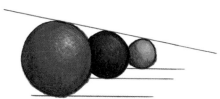

Now take at look at the guidelines we've drawn for the balls. Each one is sitting on a horizontal line or plane. And look at the diagonal slanting line. See how all the balls fit in so neatly, so proportionally?

The same thing happens when you look at a road going into the countryside. In your picture it will get smaller and thinner and lighter too! That's not what really happens to the road, it's just the way it LOOKS to our eyes as it fades into the distance.

Any time you want to draw a landscape—a street, the countryside, the beach—you'll need to use perspective.

Choose a horizon line—make sure it's horizontal—and mark its center. With a ruler or the side of a book, lightly draw straight lines on the diagonal through the center point. That point is called the vanishing point. It's where all the lines meet each other. You'll get a figure that looks just like this.

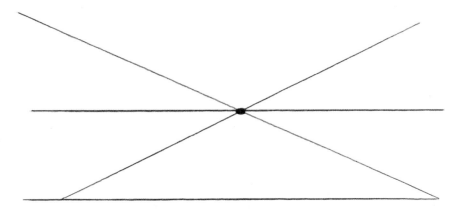

Fill in your objects so that each one fits into the space. See how the trees and the buildings get smaller and smaller. But they all stay in proportion to one another. The top line tells you how tall they should be and the bottom line tells you where they begin.

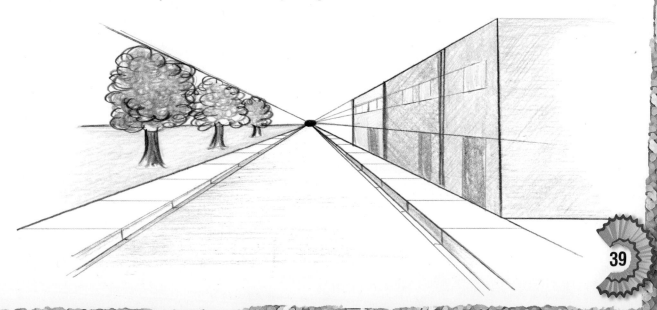

Getting out in the World

Let's put that brush and ink to the test! Can we make something beautiful—a realistic landscape filled with clouds, mountains, grass, and trees in which we can run and play (and picnic) with our friends?

DRAWING GRASS

 STEP 1: With your brush make curved strokes.

STEP 2: Keep adding grass stalks, going in the same direction, but don't make them all the same.

 STEP 3: Add some more stalks, this time vary the tone, or color, of the

DRAWING MOUNTAINS

STEP 1: With your lightest charcoal, draw a wavery, raggedy line.

STEP 2: Add a few strokes of charcoal for tone (color).

STEP 3: Add a few more strokes in crosshatch, which is a kind of criss-crossing of the lines you've drawn. Hatching is lines going one way and cross-hatching means criss-crossing lines over them.

STEP 4: Blend with your fingertips or Q-tip, but don't make it perfect. You want it to look natural.

STEP 5: Follow the same steps with the medium charcoal for middle distance.

STEP 6: Follow the same steps with darkest charcoal for nearest distance.

Remember: Things fade in color and darkness when they are farther away from us!

STEP 4: Now use a wash, and a left to right motion, add some horizontal lines to ground it.

DRAWING TREES

STEP 1: Use your pencil to start your tree. Look at a tree carefully. The branches grow outward from trunk and get skinnier and skinnier as they go. Try pressing less hard as you get to the ends so that your lines aren't so thick. That will make them look as fragile as those twigs that break off and fall to the ground!

STEP 2: For the bark, hold your pencil sideways so that you can use the side of the lead to get a broader drawing surface. Press down hard sometimes and other times less so. Make some of your lines longer and some shorter.

STEP 3: Last of all add the leaves. How big, how broad, how healthy, what kind of leaves, what color, what season? Wow! A million questions. Can you answer them? Have you even thought about them?

Use your ink, a small amount of water and your skinny brush to make leaves in a wash. Start with a light wash dabbling your leaves onto the branches and then keep adding more and more and more.

TIP: Every inch of bark looks different. Be an art scientist. Get up close and examine it. You can even take some photos to keep around for reference. Or go online and see what you can find.

Consider the Sun!

A really important element of realistic drawing is something that's not even real: SHADOWS! Here are some important things to know: shadows are formed when objects block light from the sun. Shadows are similar in shape to the objects forming them.

Shadows of objects in sunlight change over the course of the day. They are smaller when the sun is overhead and longer when the sun is closer to the ground. When the sun is overhead it lights the top of the tree. On the right, the side of the tree nearest the sun is lit and the other side is dark.

The exact same thing happens with artificial light. Just like the sun, it's the position of the objects in relation to the position of the light that determines which part of the thing will be shiny and where its shadow will fall.

It's time to put together everything you've learned! You're such an expert now, you'll have no trouble following along! Use what you've learned about shapes to add a picnic lunch to your landscape. We've broken our picnic lunch into its shapes to guide you. After lunch, you might want desert! Turn the page and find out how to draw a sweet treat!

DRAWING FROM YOUR IMAGINATION

Once you learn how to draw realistically, you can use your new skill to create a playful setting. Try putting a giant cake into a magical room. Then you can add gumdrops and lollipops for a fantasy landscape all your own!

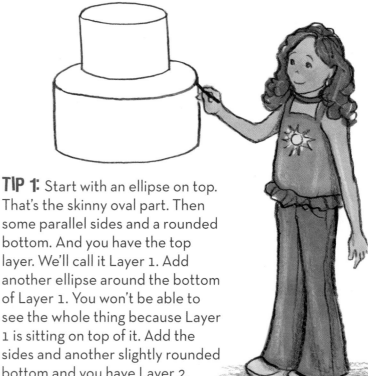

TIP 1: Start with an ellipse on top. That's the skinny oval part. Then some parallel sides and a rounded bottom. And you have the top layer. We'll call it Layer 1. Add another ellipse around the bottom of Layer 1. You won't be able to see the whole thing because Layer 1 is sitting on top of it. Add the sides and another slightly rounded bottom and you have Layer 2.

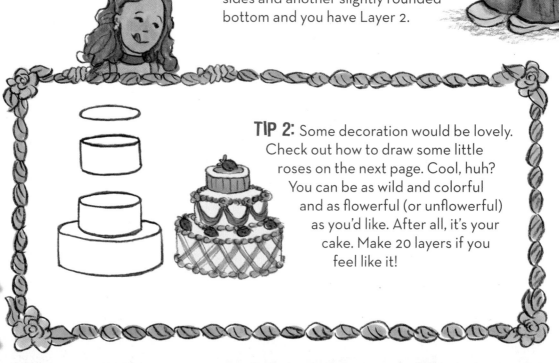

TIP 2: Some decoration would be lovely. Check out how to draw some little roses on the next page. Cool, huh? You can be as wild and colorful and as flowerful (or unflowerful) as you'd like. After all, it's your cake. Make 20 layers if you feel like it!

It's been a wonderful, day of drawing. You've learned so many things. Not just tricks and techniques, but new ways of seeing and thinking about realistic art. Your job now is to just keep learning, drawing and having fun.

After all, learning to draw IS the real thing!